Living Above Your Circumstances

Your
LIFE
WITHOUT
LIMITS

NICK VUJICIC

WATERBROOK
PRESS

YOUR LIFE WITHOUT LIMITS
PUBLISHED BY WATERBROOK PRESS
12265 Oracle Boulevard, Suite 200
Colorado Springs, Colorado 80921

This booklet has been adapted from *Life Without Limits,* copyright © 2010 by Nicholas James Vujicic.

ISBN 978-0-307-73104-3
ISBN 978-0-307-73106-7 (electronic)

Cover design by Kyle Kolker; cover photo by Aaron Hallstrom

Published in the United States by WaterBrook Multnomah, an imprint of the Crown Publishing Group, a division of Random House Inc., New York.

WATERBROOK and its deer colophon are registered trademarks of Random House Inc.

Printed in the United States of America
2013

10 9 8 7 6 5

SPECIAL SALES
Most WaterBrook Multnomah books are available at special quantity discounts when purchased in bulk by corporations, organizations, and special-interest groups. Custom imprinting or excerpting can also be done to fit special needs. For information, please e-mail SpecialMarkets@WaterBrookMultnomah.com or call 1-800-603-7051.

Your LIFE WITHOUT LIMITS

My name is Nick Vujicic (pronounced VOY-a-chich). I am twenty-nine years old. I was born without any limbs, but I am not constrained by my circumstances. I travel the world encouraging millions of people to overcome adversity with faith, hope, love, and courage so that they may pursue their dreams.

In this booklet I will share with you my experiences in dealing with adversity and obstacles, some of them unique to me but most universal to us all. My goal is to encourage you to overcome your *own* challenges and hardships so you can find your *own* purpose and pathway to a great life.

To do that well, though, you need to have hope. Why is hope so important? Where do we find it? And how do we sustain hope when life brings us hard things?

Time and again in my life and in my travels, I have witnessed the incredible power of the human spirit. I know for certain that miracles happen, but only for those who hang on to hope.

What is hope? It is where dreams begin. It is the voice of your purpose. It speaks to you and reassures you that whatever happens to you doesn't live within you. You may not control what happens to you, but you can control how you respond.

The late Reverend Martin Luther King Jr., said, "Everything that is done in the world is done by hope." I know for certain that as long as you draw breath, hope is available to you. You and I are only human. We cannot see into the future. Instead, we picture the possibilities for what might be.

Only God knows how our lives will unfold. Hope is His gift to us, a window to look through. We cannot know the future He has planned for us. Trust in Him, keep hope in your heart, and even when faced with the worst, do whatever you can to prepare yourself for the best!

Sometimes, of course, our prayers are not answered. Tragedies occur despite our prayers and our faith. Even the best people with the purest of hearts some-times suffer horrible losses and grief. The deadly earthquakes in Haiti, Chile, Mex-ico, and China are just the most re-cent examples that tremendous suffering and tragedies occur every day. Thousands died in those natural catastrophes. Their hopes and dreams died with them. Many mothers lost their children. Many chil-dren lost their mothers.

How do you sustain hope amid such suffering? One thing that sustains me when I hear of these great calamities is the fact that they always trigger incredi-ble caring from other human beings. Just when you wonder why, during such sense-less suffering, people would still have hope, hundreds of selfless volunteers pour into those regions. Students, doctors, engineers, and other rescuers and rebuilders give of themselves and their talents to help those who have survived.

Hope appears even in the worst of times to give us proof of God's presence. My own suffering seems so slight in comparison to the trials endured by so many people I've met. I've also grieved the loss of a loved one. Our family lost my cousin Roy to cancer at the age of twenty-seven, despite the fervent prayers of all the devout Christians in our family, church, and community. Losing someone so close to you is heartbreaking and difficult to understand, which is why having hope is so important to me. You see, my hope extends beyond our worldly existence.

The ultimate hope is in heaven. My family takes great consolation in the hope that my cousin, who believed in Jesus Christ, is in heaven with Him and suffering no more.

Even in the worst situations that seem beyond our capacities, God knows how much our hearts can bear. I hold on to the belief that our lives here are temporary, as we are being prepared for eternity. Whether our lives here are good or bad, the promise of heaven awaits. I always have hope in the most difficult times that God will give me the strength to endure the challenges and the heartache and that better days await, if not on this earth then for certain in heaven.

One of the best ways I've found for

holding on even when our prayers are not answered is to reach out to others. If your suffering is a burden, reach out to ease that of someone else and bring hope to him. Lift them up so that they will be comforted with the knowledge that they are not alone in their suffering. Offer compassion when you need it. Be a friend when you need friendship. Give hope when you most need it.

I am young and I don't pretend to have all the answers. More and more I realize that in those times when hopelessness seems to prevail, when our prayers go unanswered, and when our worst fears are realized, our salvation lies in our relationships with those around us and, especially for me and fellow Christians, in our relationship with God and our trust in His love and wisdom.

A POWERFUL GIFT

My belief in the power of hope over despair was reinforced on my first visit to China in 2008. I saw the Great Wall and marveled at the grandeur of one of the world's most incredible wonders. But the most powerful moment of this trip for me came when I saw the joyful glimmer in the eyes of a young Chinese girl. She was performing with other children who'd put together a show worthy of an Olympic spectacle. This girl's jubilant expression caught my attention, and I could not look away. While she moved in precision with the other dancers, she simultaneously balanced a spinning plate overhead. She was concentrating so, so hard, yet despite everything she had to think about, she still had this look of intense happiness that moved me to tears.

You see, this girl and all the children in the show were among more than four thousand young people orphaned by a massive earthquake that had hit the region just a few months earlier. My caregiver, our travel coordinator, and I had come to this orphanage with supplies for them, and I'd been asked to speak to them to raise their spirits.

As we traveled to the orphanage, I was overwhelmed by the damage and suffering caused by the earthquake. In the face of such devastation, I worried that I would not know what to tell these orphans. The earth had opened up and swallowed everything they'd loved and known. I had never endured anything so terrible. What could I say to them? We'd brought warm coats and other clothing for them, but how could I give them hope?

When I arrived at the orphanage, I was mobbed. One child after another embraced me. I didn't speak their language, but it didn't matter. Their faces said it all. Despite their circumstances, they were radiant. I should not have worried about what words to say to help them. I didn't have to inspire these children. Instead, they inspired me with the soaring spirit of their performance that day.

They'd lost their parents, their homes, and all their belongings, yet they were expressing joy.

I told them I admired their courageous spirits and urged them to keep looking forward; to dare to wish for better lives and to pursue their dreams with all their power.

DARE TO DREAM

Have the courage to pursue your own dreams, and never doubt your ability to meet whatever challenges come your way. I've seen people's amazing capacity to rise above their circumstances, not only in Chinese orphanages but in the slums of Mumbai and the prisons of Romania. I recently spoke at a social welfare center in South Korea, where some of the residents were disabled and others were single mothers. The power of their spirits amazed me.

I visited a prison in South Africa with concrete walls and rusted bars where the worst criminals were not allowed in our chapel service. I could hear voices from throughout the prison, singing along to the gospel music. It was as if the Holy Spirit had filled the entire population with God's joy. They were captive on the outside but free on the inside because of their faith and their hope. Walking out of the prison gates that day, I felt that those inmates seemed freer than many of those outside the prison gates. You too can allow hope to live in your heart.

Remember that sadness does serve a purpose. It is perfectly natural to experience this emotion, but you should never let it dominate your thoughts day and night. You can control your response by turning to more positive thoughts and actions that lift your spirits.

Because I am a spiritual person, I look to my faith in sorrowful times. But (perhaps surprisingly) it is my training in accounting that offers a more pragmatic approach. If you say you are without hope, that means you think there is *zero* chance of anything good happening in your life ever again.

Zero? That's pretty extreme, don't you think? The power of believing in better days is so indisputable that, to me, it seems far more probable that your days will change for the better. Hope, along with faith and love, is one of the pillars of spirituality. Whatever your beliefs, you should never be without hope, because everything good in life begins with it. If you didn't have hope, would you ever plan to start a family? Without hope, would you ever try to learn something new? Hope is the springboard for nearly every step we take, and my hope in writing this book is that you will find a better life.

A passage in the Bible says, "Those who hope in the LORD will renew their strength. They will soar on wings like eagles; they will run and not grow weary, they will walk and not be faint" (Isaiah

40:31). The first time I heard this passage, I realized that I didn't need arms and legs. Don't ever forget that God never gives up on you. Keep moving ahead because action creates momentum, which in turn creates unanticipated opportunities.

RIPPLES BECOME TIDES

People around the world were deeply saddened by the devastating 2010 earthquake in Haiti. Yet for all the tragedies that came with this massive disaster, the horrific circumstances also brought out people's best qualities, as in the survivors who refused to surrender despite the overwhelming odds stacked against them.

Marie's son Emmanuel was believed to

be among the dead buried under a building. The twenty-one-year-old tailor had been with his mother in her apartment when the earthquake hit. She escaped, but she could not find him afterward since the building where they lived was now just a heap of rubble. Marie looked for her son at an emergency camp set up for people who'd lost their homes, but she could not find him among the other survivors. She waited, hoping he still might make his way there.

After several days, she went back into the chaos and the destruction to search for her son. Heavy machinery at work on the site made it difficult to hear, but at one point Marie thought she heard Emmanuel calling for her.

"At that moment," she told a reporter, "I knew it was possible to save him."

Marie let everyone know that her son had called to her from under the rubble, but no one was able to help her. When groups of international rescue workers arrived, she was able to find an experienced team of engineers. She convinced them that her son was still alive. Using their equipment and knowledge, they cut through steel, concrete, and debris at exactly the spot where she'd heard her son's voice.

They kept digging until they uncovered Emmanuel's hand. He was reaching out to them. They continued until they freed his shoulder and were able to pull him out. He had been buried for ten days.

He was severely dehydrated, covered in dust, and very hungry, but he survived.

Sometimes all you have is your belief that anything is possible, that miracles can happen. As it was for Marie, the world around you may be in chaos, but you should not give in to despair. Instead, believe that whatever you lack, God will provide! That belief spurred Marie to action. Her actions brought her within reach of her son's voice. It's not a stretch to recognize that Marie's hope kept Emmanuel alive, is it?

Life may not be going well for you now, but as long as you are here, as long as you press forward, *anything* is possible.

LIVE WITH HOPE IN YOUR HEART

You may be skeptical that anything is possible by hanging on to hope. Or perhaps you have been brought down so low that finding the strength to crawl out of your despair seems impossible. There was a time when I felt exactly that way. I was absolutely convinced that my life would never be of value and that I would only be a burden to those I loved.

My parents were not prepared for a child without limbs when I was born, and as a result they were despondent. Who could blame them? Every mother and father envisions the future for the children they bring into the world. My parents had difficulty projecting what sort of future I would have, and as I grew older, so did I.

We all have, at times, seen our vision for our lives crash into a cruel reality like a car speeding into a brick wall. The particulars of your experience may be unique, but situations of despair are all too human. Teens often e-mail me stories of how abuse and neglect have ripped apart their families. Adults share stories about how drugs or alcohol or pornography have left them crippled. Some days it seems like half the people I talk to are dealing with cancer or some other life-threatening medical condition.

How do you stay hopeful in such situations? You trust in God, remember that you are here for a reason, and dedicate yourself to fulfilling that purpose. Whatever challenge you are facing, you are blessed in ways that will help you find a path through it. Just think of my parents and of the hopelessness they once faced.

BELIEVE IN THE BEST

Remaining positive and motivated when your burden feels unbearable is undoubtedly difficult. When I became old enough to understand the challenges awaiting me, I was often haunted by despair and couldn't begin to imagine that anything positive lay in store for me. My memories of the darkest days of my childhood are hazy. I was going through one of those periods when being different was particularly tough. I'm sure you have experienced those self-doubts too. We all want to fit in, but at times we all feel like outsiders.

My insecurities and doubts sprang mostly from the physical challenges of having no arms or legs. I cannot know what your concerns are, but hanging on to hope helped me. Here is just one early experience of how it worked in my world:

I was just a toddler when my medical team recommended that my parents put me in a play group with other kids labeled "disabled." Their challenges ranged from missing limbs to cystic fibrosis and severe mental disorders. My parents had great love and empathy for other special-needs kids and their families, but they didn't think any child should be limited to one group of playmates.

They held on to the conviction that my life would have no limits, and they fought to keep that dream alive.

My mother, bless her, made an important decision at an early stage of my life. "Nicholas, you need to play with normal children because you are normal. You just have a few bits and pieces missing, that's all," she said, setting the tone for years to come. She didn't want me to feel less than normal or restricted in any way. She didn't want me to become introverted, shy, or insecure just because I was different physically.

Little did I realize that my parents, even then, were instilling in me the belief that I had every right to a life free of labels and restrictions.

You have that right too. You should demand to be free of whatever categorizations or limits others try to put on you. Because of my missing "bits and pieces," I am sensitive to the fact that some people accept what others say about them and even unconsciously restrict themselves. There certainly were times I was tired or cranky and tried to claim that studying or going to the doctor was just too taxing, but my parents refused to let me hide behind that.

Labels can provide a tempting hiding place. Some people use them as excuses; others rise above them. Many, many people have been labeled "handicapped" or "disabled" only to soar above, enjoying dynamic lives and doing important things. I encourage you to rise above any attempt to restrict you from exploring and developing your gifts.

As a child of God, I know that He is always with me, and I'm comforted to know that He understands how much we can bear.

When others share stories with me of their own challenges and trials, I'm often moved to tears. I remind those who are suffering or grieving that God's arm is never too short. He can reach anyone.

Draw strength from that. Dare to give it a go and to soar as high as your imagination will take you. You can expect challenges. Welcome them as character-building experiences. Learn from them and rise above them. You may have an excellent dream. Just be open-minded enough to accept that God may have a different path for you than the one you envisioned. There are many ways to reach your dream, so don't be discouraged if you can't yet see the way on your own.

BIONIC BOY

Hope is a catalyst. It can even move obstacles that seem immovable. When you keep pushing and refusing to give up, you create momentum. Hope creates opportunities you never would have anticipated. Helpful people are drawn to you. Doors open. Paths are cleared.

Remember—action brings reaction. When you are tempted to abandon your dreams, push yourself to continue one more day, one more week, one more month, and one more year. You will be amazed at what happens when you refuse to quit.

When it came time for me to begin elementary school, my parents again lobbied for me to have a typical education. As a result of their unyielding conviction, I became one of the first disabled children in Australia to mainstream into the regular school system.

I did so well in the mainstream school that the local newspaper ran a story with the headline: "Integration Lets Disabled Boy Blossom."

The story, accompanied by a big photograph of my sister, Michelle, riding with me in my wheelchair, set off a national media blitz that brought visits from government officials, cards, letters, gifts, and invitations from across the country.

The donations that flowed in after that newspaper story helped fund my parents' efforts to equip me with replacement limbs. They'd been trying to fit me with artificial limbs since I was eighteen months old. My first prosthesis was just one arm, which didn't work well for me. The arm and hand were operated mechanically with pulleys and levers, and it weighed about twice as much as all the rest of me! Just keeping my balance with this contraption on was a challenge. I managed to operate it after a while. I'd already become adept at grabbing objects with my little foot, my chin, or my teeth, so the bionic arm seemed only to make daily chores more difficult.

My parents were disappointed at first, but my confidence grew because I felt good about doing so well on my own. I encouraged them and thanked them and looked ahead.

There is power in perseverance. Our first experiment with an artificial limb failed, but I continued to believe my life would work out for the best. My optimism and high spirits inspired our community Lions Club, an international service organization, to raise more than $200,000 for my medical bills and a new wheelchair.

Some of those funds also helped us travel to Toronto, Canada, to try a more advanced set of electronic arms developed by a children's clinic. In the end, however, even the medical experts decided that I managed to accomplish most tasks more efficiently on my own without the aid of prosthetics.

I was excited that there were scientists and inventors intent on providing me with limbs someday. But I became all the more determined to do whatever I could without waiting for someone else to find something that would improve my life—I had to find my own answers. Even today I welcome anyone who helps me, whether it is opening a door for my wheelchair or giving me a drink from a glass of water. We need to take responsibility for our own happiness and success. Your friends and family may reach out to you in times of need. Be grateful for that. Welcome their efforts, but keep pushing on your own too. The more effort you put into it, the more opportunities you create.

Sometimes you may feel as if you are just about to realize your goal only to fall short. That is no reason to quit. Defeat happens only to those who refuse to try again. I still believe that one day I will be able to walk and lift and hold utensils like a regular person.

It will be a miracle when that happens, whether God does it on His own or through His agents on earth. The technology for robotic limbs is advancing rapidly. Someday I may be able to wear prosthetic arms and legs that work efficiently, but for now I'm happy to be just as I am.

Often the very challenges that we think are holding us back are, in fact, making us stronger. You should be open to the possibility that today's handicap might be tomorrow's advantage. I've come to see my lack of limbs as an asset. Men, women, and children who can't speak my language only have to see me to know that I have overcome many challenges. My lessons, they know, did not come easily.

WISDOM BORN OF EXPERIENCE

When I tell my audiences to hold on for better days, I speak from experience. You can believe and trust in what I say because I have been there. At one point in my life, I gave up hope.

This low point in my mostly happy childhood came around the age of ten, when negative thoughts overwhelmed me. No matter how optimistic and determined and inventive I tried to be, there were some tasks I just could not do. Some of them were simple, everyday activities. It really bothered me, for example, that I couldn't grab a soda out of the refrigerator like every other kid. I couldn't feed

myself, and I hated to ask other people to
do it. I felt bad that they had to interrupt
their meals to help me. Other, bigger
issues haunted me in this period of my
life: Would I ever find a wife to love me?
How would I provide for her and our children? How could I protect them if they
were threatened?

Most people have such thoughts. You
probably have wondered at some point
whether you would ever have a lasting
relationship, a secure job, or a safe place
to live. It is normal and healthy to look
ahead because that is how we develop a
vision for our lives. The problem comes
when negative thoughts block your
vision for the future and cloud your
mind. I pray and I remind myself of the

Word of God, who helps me know that He is with me. He never leaves me. He hasn't forgotten me. He will cause even the worst things to come together for the good. I remind myself to hold on to the promises of God, no matter what I see on the outside. I know that God is good. If He allows something bad to happen, I may not understand, but I can hold on to His goodness.

MONITOR YOUR THOUGHTS

As my eleventh birthday approached, I entered the tricky adolescent stage when our brains rewire and strange chemicals flow through out bodies. Other boys and girls my age were starting to pair up, which added to my growing sense of alienation. *Would any girl ever want a boyfriend who couldn't hold her hand or dance with her?*

Without even being aware of it, I allowed those dark thoughts and negative feelings to burden my spirit with growing frequency. Often they came creeping into my mind late at night when I couldn't sleep or when I was tired after a long day at school. You know the feeling; you are so weary and out of sorts that the whole world seems to be weighing on your shoulders. We all experience down times, especially when lack of sleep, illness, and other challenges make us vulnerable.

No one is happy and perky one hundred percent of the time. Your more somber moods are natural. They serve a purpose too. According to recent psychological studies, a darker mood can make you look at your work more critically and analytically. That outlook is helpful when you are involved in tasks such as balancing your checkbook, figuring out your taxes, or editing a paper. As long as you are aware of and in control of your emotions, negative thoughts can produce positive consequences. Only when you let your emotions control your actions do you risk spiraling down into depression and self-destructive behaviors.

The key is to refuse to be overwhelmed or swept away by negative emotions or feelings of depression. Fortunately, you have that power to adjust your attitude.

When you detect negative thoughts running through your mind, you can choose to hit the off switch. Acknowledge them and understand their source, but stay focused on the solutions instead of on the problems.

I remember from Bible class a picture of the whole "armor of God" with the breastplate of righteousness, the belt of truth, the shield of faith, the sword of the Spirit, and the helmet of salvation. I'd learned that those were all the weapons that a Christian boy would ever need. I see the Word of God as a sword to fight negative thoughts. The sword is the Bible. You also hold up the shield of faith to defend yourself.

SPIRAL OF DESPAIR

At that critical point when entering adolescence when self-esteem and self-image are so important, I let my worries and fears overtake me. Everything that was wrong with me overpowered all that was right. *I drew the short straw. How will I ever lead a normal life with a job, a wife, and kids? I will always be a burden to those around me.*

I was never crippled until I lost hope. Believe me, the loss of hope is far worse than the loss of limbs. If you have ever experienced grief or depression, you know just how bad despair can be. More than ever I felt angry, hurt, and confused.

I prayed, asking God why He couldn't give me what He'd given everyone else. *Did I do something wrong? Is that why You don't answer my prayers for arms and legs? Why won't You help me? Why do You make me suffer?*

Neither God nor my doctors could explain to me why I'd been born without arms or legs. The lack of an explanation, even a scientific one, only made me feel worse. I kept thinking that if there was some reason, spiritual, medical, or otherwise, it might be easier to handle. The pain might not be so great.

Many times I felt so low that I refused to go to school. Self-pity hadn't been a problem before. I had been constantly striving to overcome my disability, to do normal activities, to play as other kids played. Most of the time I impressed my parents, my teachers, and my classmates with my determination and self-sufficiency. Yet inside I harbored hurt.

I'd been raised as a spiritual kid. I'd always gone to church and believed in prayer and God's healing power. I was so into Jesus that when we had dinner, I'd smile, thinking of Him with us there at the table, sitting in our empty chair while we ate. I prayed for arms and legs. For a while I expected to wake up some morning with arms and legs. I'd settle for just getting one arm or leg at a time. When they did not appear, I grew angry with God.

I thought I'd figured out God's purpose

in creating me, which was to be His partner in a miracle so the world would recognize that He was real. I would pray: "God, if You gave me arms and legs, I would go around the world and share the miracle. I would go on national television and tell everyone what had happened, and the world would see the power of God." I was telling Him that I got it and was willing to follow through on my end. I remember praying, *God, I know You made me this way so You could give me arms and legs and the miracle would prove to people Your power and love.*

As a child, I learned that God speaks to us in many ways. I felt He might answer me by placing a feeling in my heart. But there was only silence. I felt nothing.

My parents would tell me, "Only God knows why you were born this way." Then I'd ask God, and He wouldn't tell me. These unfulfilled appeals and unanswered questions hurt me deeply because I had felt so close to God before.

I had other challenges to face. We were moving a thousand miles north, up the coast to Queensland, Australia, away from my huge family.

My protective cocoon of aunts and uncles and twenty-six cousins was being stripped away. The stress of moving was wearing on my parents too. Despite their assurances and their love and support, I couldn't shake the feeling that I was a tremendous burden to them.

It was as though I'd put on dark blinders

that prevented me from seeing any light in my life. I couldn't see how I would ever be of use to anyone. I felt I was just a mistake, a freak of nature, God's forgotten child. My dad and mum did their best to tell me otherwise. They read to me from the Bible. They took me to church. My Sunday school teachers taught that God loves us all. But I couldn't move beyond my pain and anger.

There were brighter moments. In Sunday school I felt joy when I joined my classmates singing, "Jesus loves the little children, all the children of the world, red and yellow, black and white, all are precious in His sight, Jesus loves the little children of the world." Surrounded by people who supported and loved me, I took that hymn to heart. It comforted me.

I wanted to believe that He cared for me deeply, but when I was tired or not feeling well, the dark thoughts would creep in. I'd sit in my wheelchair on the playground wondering: *If God really loves me like all the other children, then why didn't He give me arms and legs? Why did He make me so different from His other children?*

Those thoughts began to intrude even during the day and in normally happy circumstances. I'd been struggling with feelings of despair and the sense that my life was always going to be difficult. God didn't seem to answer my prayers.

One day I sat on the high kitchen countertop, watching my loving mum cook dinner, which I usually found reassuring and relaxing. But suddenly these negative thoughts overcame me. It struck me that I didn't want to stick around and be a burden to her. I had the urge to throw myself off the counter. I looked down.

I tried to work out what angle I should use to make sure I snapped my neck and killed myself.

But I talked myself out of doing it, mostly because if I failed to kill myself, I'd have to explain why I was in such despair. The fact that I came so close to hurting myself that way frightened me. I should have told my mother what I'd been thinking, but I was embarrassed. I didn't want to scare her.

I was young, and even though I was surrounded by people who loved me, I didn't reach out and tell them the depth of my feelings. I had resources but didn't use them, and that was a mistake.

If you feel overcome by dark moods, you don't have to handle it yourself. Those who love you won't feel burdened. They *want* to help you. If you feel you can't confide in them, reach out to professional counselors at school, at work, or in your community. You are not alone. I was not alone. I see that now, and I don't want you to ever come as close as I did to making a fatal mistake.

But at that time I was becoming swept

up in hopelessness. I decided that to end my pain, I had to end my life.

A CLOSE CALL

One afternoon after school I asked my mother if she could put me in the bath to soak for a while. I asked her to shut the door when she left the bathroom. Then I put my ears under water. In the silence, very heavy thoughts ran through my mind. I had planned in advance what I wanted to do.

If God will not take away my pain, and if there is no purpose for me in this life...if I'm here only to experience rejection and loneliness...I'm a burden to everyone and I have no future... I should just end it now.

When I learned how to swim, I'd float on my back by filling my lungs with air. Now I tried to gauge how much air to keep in my lungs before I flipped over. *Do I hold my breath before I turn over? Do I take a full deep breath, or do I just do half? Should I just empty my lungs and flip over?*

I finally just turned and plunged my face under water. Instinctively, I held my breath. Because my lungs were strong, I stayed afloat for what seemed like a long time.

When my air gave out, I flipped back over.

I can't do this.

But the dark thoughts persisted: *I want to get out of here. I just want to disappear.* I blew most of the air out of my lungs and flipped over again. I knew I could hold my breath for at least ten seconds, so I counted down: 10...9...8...7...6...5...4...3...

As I counted, an image flashed in my mind of my dad and mum standing at my grave crying. I saw my seven-year-old brother, Aaron, crying too. They were all weeping, saying it was their fault, that they should have done more for me.

I couldn't stand the thought of leaving them feeling responsible for my death for the rest of their lives.

I'm being selfish.

I flipped back over and drew a deep breath. I couldn't do it. I couldn't leave my family with such a burden of loss and guilt.

But my anguish was unbearable. That night in our shared bedroom, I told Aaron, "I'm planning to commit suicide when I'm twenty-one."

I thought I could stick it out through high school and university maybe, but I couldn't see myself beyond that. I didn't feel like I could ever get a job or get married like other men. What woman would want to marry me? So the age of twenty-one seemed like the end of the road for me. At my age, of course, it also seemed like a long time away.

"I'm telling Dad you said that," my little brother replied.

I told him not to tell anyone and closed my eyes to sleep. The next thing I knew, I felt the weight of my father as he sat down on my trundle bed.

"What is this about you wanting to kill yourself?" he asked.

In a warm and reassuring tone, he talked to me about all the good things awaiting me. As he spoke, he combed my hair with his fingers. I always loved it when he did that.

"We will always be here for you," he reassured me. "Everything is going to be okay. I promise we will always be here for you. You are going to be fine, son."

A loving touch and caring gaze is sometimes all it takes to put a child's troubled heart and confused mind at ease. My father's reassurance that things would be okay was enough in that moment. He convinced me with his comforting tone and touch that he believed we would find a path for me. Every son wants to trust his father, and that night he gave me something to hold on to. To a child, there is no assurance like a father's. My dad was generous with such things and good at expressing his love and support for all of us.

I still didn't understand how everything would work out for me, but because my daddy told me it would, I believed it would.

I slept soundly after our talk. I still had occasional bad days and nights. I trusted my parents and held on to hope for a long time before I actually formed any vision of how my life might unfold. There were moments and even longer periods of doubt and fear, but fortunately this was the lowest point for me.

Even now I have my down times like anyone else, but I never again considered suicide. When I look back on that moment and reflect on my life since, I can only thank God for rescuing me from my despair.

HOLDING ON TO HOPE

Through my speaking engagements in twenty-four countries, DVDs, and millions of YouTube.com views, I've been blessed to reach so many with a message of hope. Think about just how much joy I would have missed experiencing if I had taken my life at the age of ten. I would have missed the extraordinary opportunity of sharing my story and what I'd learned with more than 120,000 people in India, another 18,000 in a bullring in Colombia, and 9,000 during a thunderstorm in Ukraine.

In time I came to understand that even though I didn't take my life that dark day, *God did.*

He took my life and gave it more meaning and more purpose and more joy than a ten-year-old boy could ever have understood.

Don't you make the mistake I nearly made.

If I had remained facedown in six inches of water back in 1993, I might have ended my temporary pain, but at what cost? That despairing child could not possibly have foreseen the joyful man swimming with great sea turtles off the Hawaiian coast, surfing in California, or scuba diving in Colombia.

Even more important than those adventures are the many lives I might never have touched. I'm just one small example.

Pick any true-life hero, whether it's Mother Teresa, Mahatma Gandhi, or Dr. Martin Luther King Jr., and you'll find someone who had to weather adversity—prison, violence, even the threat of death—

but held on to the belief that his dreams could prevail.

When negative thoughts and dark moods come to you, remember that you have a choice. If you need help, reach out for it. You are not alone. You can choose to picture better days and to perform actions that will make them real.

Consider what I was up against as a boy and look at my life now. Who knows what great days and wonderful achievements await you? Who knows how many lives we can make better by serving as someone else's miracle?

So walk with me, the man with no arms and no legs, into a future filled with hope!

READ THE STORY BEHIND THE INSPIRATIONAL MESSAGE.

Telling his story of learning to live with his physical limitations, Nick Vujicic offers practical advice applicable to everyone looking for a life of fulfillment and happiness.

Read an excerpt at www.WaterBrookMultnomah.com.